L137

Safe maintenance, repair and cleaning procedures

Dangerous Substances and
Explosive Atmospheres Regulations 2002

APPROVED CODE OF PRACTICE
AND GUIDANCE

HSE BOOKS

© *Crown copyright 2003*

First published 2003

ISBN 0 7176 2202 9

All rights reserved. No part of this publication may be reproduced, stored in a retrieval system, or transmitted in any form or by any means (electronic, mechanical, photocopying, recording or otherwise) without the prior written permission of the copyright owner.

Applications for reproduction should be made in writing to:
Licensing Division, Her Majesty's Stationery Office,
St Clements House, 2-16 Colegate, Norwich NR3 1BQ
or by e-mail to hmsolicensing@cabinet-office.x.gsi.gov.uk

This Code has been approved by the Health and Safety Commission, with the consent of the Secretary of State. It gives practical advice on how to comply with the law. If you follow the advice you will be doing enough to comply with the law in respect of those specific matters on which the Code gives advice. You may use alternative methods to those set out in the Code in order to comply with the law.

However, the Code has special legal status. If you are prosecuted for breach of health and safety law, and it is proved that you did not follow the relevant provisions of the Code, you will need to show that you have complied with the law in some other way or a court will find you at fault.

The extract of the Regulations and the Approved Code of Practice (ACOP) are accompanied by guidance which does not form part of the ACOP. Following the guidance is not compulsory and you are free to take other action. But if you do follow the guidance you will normally be doing enough to comply with the law. Health and Safety inspectors seek to secure compliance with the law and may refer to this guidance as illustrating good practice.

Contents

Preface *iv*

Notice of Approval *v*

Introduction *1*

Regulation 5 - Assessment of the risks *3*
Dangerous substances as a result of work activity *4*

Regulation 6 (and Schedule 1) - Elimination or reduction of risks from dangerous substances *5*
Eliminating dangerous substances from plant and work areas *7*
Systems of work *8*
Permit-to-work *10*
Activities involving hot work *12*

References and further reading *17*

Preface

This publication contains an extract from the Dangerous Substances and Explosive Atmospheres Regulations[1] (regulations 5 and 6 and Schedule 1), together with an Approved Code of Practice and supporting guidance.

For convenience, the text of the Regulations is set out in *italic* type, with the ACOP in **bold** type and the accompanying guidance in normal type.

Notice of Approval

By virtue of section 16(1) of the Health and Safety at Work etc Act 1974 and with the consent of the Secretary of State for Work and Pensions, the Health and Safety Commission has on 13 May 2003 approved the Code of Practice entitled *Safe maintenance, repair and cleaning procedures*.

The Code of Practice gives practical guidance with respect to regulations 5 and 6 of the Dangerous Substances and Explosive Atmospheres Regulations 2002 with regard to safe maintenance, repair and cleaning procedures where dangerous substances are or may be present.

The Code of Practice comes into effect on 27 October 2003.

Signed

MARK DEMPSEY
Secretary to the Health and Safety Commission
3 October 2003

Introduction

1   The Dangerous Substances and Explosive Atmospheres Regulations 2002[1] (DSEAR) are concerned with protection against risks from fire, explosion and similar events arising from dangerous substances used or present in the workplace. They set minimum requirements for the protection of workers from fire and explosion risks related to dangerous substances and potentially explosive atmospheres. The Regulations apply to employers and the self-employed and apply at most workplaces in Great Britain where a dangerous substance is, or could be, present.

2   DSEAR revokes, repeals or modifies a large amount of old legislation relating to flammable substances and dusts. Safety standards will be maintained through a combination of the requirements of DSEAR and ACOPs (Approved Codes of Practice) reflecting good practices in the old legislation.[2-6]

3   The key requirements in DSEAR are that risks from dangerous substances are assessed and eliminated or reduced. This ACOP provides practical advice on what employers need to do to meet the requirements of regulations 5 and 6 of DSEAR (on assessment and control of risks) at places where maintenance, repair and cleaning activities are carried out. It also provides advice on appropriate systems of work and details permit-to-work procedures for hot work and other activities that are identified as high risk.

4   This publication is part of a series of publications intended to support DSEAR. Other activity-related ACOP and guidance material is available in the following publications:

(a) *Dangerous substances and explosive atmospheres*[2] - This provides an overview of how employers can meet their duties under DSEAR.

(b) *Design of plant, equipment and workplaces*[3] - This gives practical advice on assessing the risk from, and the design and use of, plant, equipment and workplaces which handle or process dangerous substances. It includes measures for making redundant plant and equipment safe.

(c) *Storage of dangerous substances*[4] - This gives practical advice on the requirements of regulation 5 and 6 to assess the risks from, and the control and mitigation measures for, places where dangerous substances are stored. It includes the safe disposal of waste materials.

(d) *Control and mitigation measures*[5] - This gives practical advice on the requirements of regulation 5 and 6 to identify the hazards arising from the dangerous substance and put in place adequate ventilation, ignition control and separation measures to control risks.

(e) *Unloading petrol from road tankers*[6] - This gives practical advice and contains a code of practice in respect to regulation 6 with regard to the safe unloading of petrol tankers at petrol filling stations.

5   In addition, the free leaflet *Fire and explosion - How safe is your workplace?*[7] provides a short guide to DSEAR and is aimed at small and medium sized businesses.

6   Information on DSEAR can also be accessed via HSE's website: www.hse.gov.uk, which is regularly updated.

Regulation 5

Regulation

Assessment of the risks

(1) Where a dangerous substance is or is liable to be present at the workplace, the employer shall make a suitable and sufficient assessment of the risks to his employees which arise from that substance.

(2) The risk assessment shall include consideration of -

(a) the hazardous properties of the substance;

(b) information on safety provided by the supplier, including information contained in any relevant safety data sheet;

(c) the circumstances of the work including -

    (i) the work processes and substances used and their possible interactions;

    (ii) the amount of the substance involved;

    (iii) where the work will involve more than one dangerous substance, the risk presented by such substances in combination; and

    (iv) the arrangements for the safe handling, storage and transport of dangerous substances and of waste containing dangerous substances;

(d) activities, such as maintenance, where there is the potential for a high level of risk;

(e) the effect of measures which have been or will be taken pursuant to these Regulations;

(f) the likelihood that an explosive atmosphere will occur and its persistence;

(g) the likelihood that ignition sources, including electrostatic discharges, will be present and become active and effective;

(h) the scale of the anticipated effects of a fire or an explosion;

(i) any places which are or can be connected via openings to places in which explosive atmospheres may occur; and

(j) such additional safety information as the employer may need in order to complete the risk assessment.

ACOP

7   Employers must carry out a risk assessment before:

(a) any maintenance, repair, modification, extension, restructuring, demolition or cleaning activities are undertaken in areas where dangerous substances are used, stored or produced;

(b) any maintenance, repair, modification, extension, restructuring, demolition or cleaning activities are undertaken on any plant or equipment that has contained a dangerous substance; or

(c) using any dangerous substance for any maintenance, repair or cleaning activity.

ACOP

8 In carrying out the assessment employers will need to identify:

(a) the fire and explosion hazards arising from the proposed work;

(b) the necessary control and mitigation measures so that the work can be carried out safely; and

(c) the appropriate system of work to ensure that the control and mitigation measures essential for safety are properly understood and implemented.

Guidance

9 Factors which should be considered in the assessment for any maintenance, repair, modification, extension, restructuring, demolition or cleaning activities include:

(a) the materials that are being used or may have been used in the area or plant where the activity is to be carried out;

(b) which materials are dangerous substances or may become hazardous under the conditions of the proposed work (including residues or by-products that may occur or build up inside plant or any materials that could be released by the proposed activity - see paragraph 12);

(c) potential heat or ignition sources that may arise during the proposed activity;

(d) how and where explosive atmospheres can arise;

(e) the consequences of a fire or explosion during the activity;

(f) the basis of safety during the proposed activity - see paragraph 10;

(g) the training and level of competence required by the operatives;

(h) what additional protective and emergency equipment is required; and

(i) what systems of work will be needed to implement the necessary control measures during the proposed activity - see paragraph 23.

10 In deciding how safety is to be maintained the employer should decide whether dangerous substances and any associated explosive atmospheres need to be removed from the plant and work area, or whether they can be rendered safe temporarily by inerting or ventilation techniques. The employer will also need to decide whether ignition sources can be allowed into the work area on a temporary basis.

ACOP

Dangerous substances as a result of work activity

11 When assessing risks, employers must take into account the types of dangerous substances that may be present. This must include substances that could become dangerous as a result of the work activity itself or that may be generated by the activity.

Guidance

12 Groups of materials or residues that would be defined as dangerous substances as a result of heat applied or arising during hot work include:

(a) combustible liquids with a flashpoint above 55°C but below the temperature of the hot work during which they can evaporate to give rise to an explosive atmosphere (eg diesel fuel or olive oil);

Guidance

(b) practically non-flammable materials - these are substances which are almost, but not quite, non-flammable. They include materials that are difficult to ignite and will not burn under normal conditions but which can be ignited by a powerful ignition source, such as a welding torch. Most organic materials that are not classified as either flammable or combustible will be included in this group (eg methylene chloride);

(c) flammable dusts which may be dispersed to give rise to an explosive atmosphere or cause latent smouldering hazards (eg wood dust);

(d) any substance that can decompose under the conditions of the hot work to give off flammable components which may then give rise to an explosive atmosphere (eg rubbers or plastics); and

(e) any substance that can decompose under the conditions of the hot work to give rise to hazardous heat or pressure effects (eg dinitrotoluene or sodium hydrosulphite or residues and by-products from reactions and other similar processes).

13 Employers will also need to assess risks to workers' health that may arise from maintenance operations and other similar activities under the Control of Substances Hazardous to Health Regulations 2002 (COSHH).[8]

Regulation 6

Elimination or reduction of risks from dangerous substances

Regulation

(1) Every employer shall ensure that risk is either eliminated or reduced so far as is reasonably practicable.

(2) In complying with his duty under paragraph (1), substitution shall by preference be undertaken, whereby the employer shall avoid, so far as is reasonably practicable, the presence or use of a dangerous substance at the workplace by replacing it with a substance or process which either eliminates or reduces the risk.

(3) Where it is not reasonably practicable to eliminate risk pursuant to paragraphs (1) and (2), the employer shall, so far as is reasonably practicable, apply measures, consistent with the risk assessment and appropriate to the nature of the activity or operation -

(a) to control risks, including the measures specified in paragraph (4); and

(b) to mitigate the detrimental effects of a fire or explosion or the other harmful physical effects arising from dangerous substances, including the measures specified in paragraph (5).

(4) The following measures are, in order of priority, those specified for the purposes of paragraph (3)(a) -

(a) the reduction of the quantity of dangerous substances to a minimum;

(b) the avoidance or minimising of the release of a dangerous substance;

(c) the control of the release of a dangerous substance at source;

(d) the prevention of the formation of an explosive atmosphere, including the application of appropriate ventilation;

Regulation 6

(e) ensuring that any release of a dangerous substance which may give rise to risk is suitably collected, safely contained, removed to a safe place, or otherwise rendered safe, as appropriate;

(f) the avoidance of -

   (i) ignition sources including electrostatic discharges; and

   (ii) adverse conditions which could cause dangerous substances to give rise to harmful physical effects; and

(g) the segregation of incompatible dangerous substances.

(5) The following measures are those specified for the purposes of paragraph (3)(b) -

(a) the reduction to a minimum of the number of employees exposed;

(b) the avoidance of the propagation of fires or explosions;

(c) the provision of explosion pressure relief arrangements;

(d) the provision of explosion suppression equipment;

(e) the provision of plant which is constructed so as to withstand the pressure likely to be produced by an explosion; and

(f) the provision of suitable personal protective equipment.

(6) The employer shall arrange for the safe handling, storage and transport of dangerous substances and waste containing dangerous substances.

(7) The employer shall ensure that any conditions necessary pursuant to these Regulations for ensuring the elimination or reduction of risk are maintained.

(8) The employer shall, so far as is reasonably practicable, take the general safety measures specified in Schedule 1, subject to those measures being consistent with the risk assessment and appropriate to the nature of the activity or operation.

Schedule 1

General safety measures

1. The following measures are those specified for the purposes of regulation 6(8).

Workplace and work processes

2. Ensuring that the workplace is designed, constructed and maintained so as to reduce risk.

3. Designing, constructing, assembling, installing, providing and using suitable work processes so as to reduce risk.

4. Maintaining work processes in an efficient state, in efficient working order and in good repair.

5. Ensuring that equipment and protective systems meet the following requirements -

Schedule

(a) *where power failure can give rise to the spread of additional risk, equipment and protective systems must be able to be maintained in a safe state of operation independently of the rest of the plant in the event of power failure;*

(b) *means for manual override must be possible, operated by employees competent to do so, for shutting down equipment and protective systems incorporated within automatic processes which deviate from the intended operating conditions, provided that the provision or use of such means does not compromise safety;*

(c) *on operation of emergency shutdown, accumulated energy must be dissipated as quickly and as safely as possible or isolated so that it no longer constitutes a hazard; and*

(d) *necessary measures must be taken to prevent confusion between connecting devices.*

Organisational measures

6. *The application of appropriate systems of work including -*

(a) *the issuing of written instructions for the carrying out of the work; and*

(b) *a system of permits to work with such permits being issued by a person with responsibility for this function prior to the commencement of the work concerned,*

where the work is carried out in hazardous places or involves hazardous activities.

ACOP

Eliminating dangerous substances from plant and work areas

14 Employers should, where reasonably practicable, remove dangerous substances and prevent the occurrence of explosive atmospheres in areas before any maintenance, repair, modification, extension, restructuring, demolition or cleaning activities are carried out.

Guidance

15 Eliminating dangerous substances will include removing stocks of dangerous substances, cleaning and making plant safe, sealing drums and containers, isolating pipework or material handling systems and clearing up any spills or deposits of dangerous substances.

Cleaning tanks, plant and other equipment

16 The employer should ensure that risks are assessed and appropriate control measures are identified before cleaning tanks, plant and equipment.

17 Isolating and cleaning plant and equipment is a hazardous activity and as well as considering the factors listed in paragraph 9 the employer will also, where necessary, need to implement measures to:

(a) isolate plant and equipment from sources of dangerous substances;

(b) control ignition sources in any additional hazardous zones created by the work;

(c) establish acceptable concentrations of dangerous substances for particular work activities;

Guidance

(d) monitor the concentration of dangerous substances within the plant and in the surrounding area;

(e) maintain concentrations of dangerous substances below predetermined safe limits by ventilation or inerting techniques;

(f) establish action limits and procedures should the predetermined limits be exceeded during cleaning work; and

(g) ensure that the plant or equipment is inspected by a competent person and is declared clean and safe for the intended work.

18   Where entry into tanks or plant is required the employer will also need to take into account the requirements of the Confined Spaces Regulations 1997.[9]

ACOP

19   Where it is necessary to work with a dangerous substance regulation 6 requires employers, so far as is reasonably practicable, to implement measures to control the risks and to mitigate the consequences of any fire or explosion that could arise.

20   Where it is not reasonably practicable to remove dangerous substances from the work area, plant or equipment concerned, employers should determine, from the assessment, the measures that are necessary to control the risks from fire or explosion. These will include:

(a) minimising the presence and avoiding releases of dangerous substances;

(b) preventing the occurrence of explosive atmospheres by inerting or adequate ventilation;

(c) preventing ignition sources from being introduced into the work area; and

(d) providing appropriate emergency arrangements and equipment.

Guidance

Dangerous substances used as cleaning agents

21   The use of dangerous substances for cleaning purposes should be avoided wherever possible. Where it is necessary the employer should ensure that a substance with the least hazardous properties is selected.

22   For manual cleaning operations use of a dangerous substance should be minimised by applying it to an article or surface in small sections at a time. Employers will need to ensure that there is adequate ventilation of the work area and that ignition sources are eliminated. Properly designed safety containers should be used to handle and dispense dangerous substances.

23   Where dangerous substances are introduced into plant or equipment for cleaning purposes employers should ensure that any additional hazards, including their compatibility with other dangerous substances present, are identified and appropriate control measures are implemented.

ACOP

Systems of work

24   Regulation 6 and Schedule 1 require employers, so far as is reasonably practicable, to take measures consistent with the risk assessment and appropriate to the operation, including:

ACOP

(a) the design, construction, assembly, installation, provision and use of suitable work processes; and

(b) the use of systems of work, including permit-to-work systems, to control the hazards and potential hazards arising from work in areas where dangerous substances are present or during work activities that involve dangerous substances.

25 Employers should ensure that the system of work, identified from their risk assessment, is properly implemented before any maintenance, repair, modification, extension, restructuring, demolition or cleaning activities are carried out.

Guidance

26 The system of work should ensure that the control measures necessary for a particular activity are properly understood and implemented and that an appropriate level of control is in place. The level of control required will depend on the risks associated with the activity and may be based on simple operating procedures, safety method statements or a permit-to-work system. In deciding on an appropriate system of work the employer will also need to take into account other health and safety issues that may arise during the proposed work. These include exposure to toxic or corrosive chemicals, electric shock hazards, high pressure systems, hazards from moving machinery, burns from hot (and cold) materials and safe access.

Operating procedures for low risk activities

27 For low risk activities employers should ensure that adequate control measures are implemented through adequate supervision or a system of work that may include the use of written operating procedures.

28 Such activities do not increase the level of risk associated with the work normally carried out in that area. They do not, for example, introduce ignition sources into the work area or create a risk of releasing dangerous materials. They may include:

(a) routine cleaning operations;

(b) dealing with small leaks and spills during normal manufacturing or handling operations; and

(c) routine machine and equipment adjustments.

29 Employers should identify the risks prior to the work and where necessary incorporate the control measures into written operating procedures.

Safety method statements

30 For medium risk activities the employer should ensure that appropriate control measures are implemented through the use of safety method statements.

31 Medium risk activities include maintenance, repair and servicing activities carried out by employees and contractors within or near to hazardous areas or on plant or equipment containing a dangerous substance. They may involve work that releases small quantities of dangerous substances but they should not have the potential to release a significant quantity. A significant quantity is considered to be one that could create explosive atmospheres beyond the hazardous areas already designated for the installation or one that

Guidance

could affect the health and safety of others on or off the site. Medium risk activities do not introduce ignition sources into hazardous areas.

32 Such activities may include:

(a) leak testing of tanks and lines; or

(b) hot work in areas where there are only small quantities of dangerous substances present that do not give rise to hazardous places, for example laboratories or motor vehicle workshops (but see paragraph 36(a)).

33 A safety method statement is a written procedure to cover a particular non-routine task. As well as specifying the work to be done it will also identify the hazards associated with the work and the measures necessary to control those hazards. For repetitive tasks a generic safety method statement can be used and, where necessary, modified to take into account job specific requirements or deviations. Safety method statements are inappropriate for high risk activities which should be subject to a permit-to-work system (see paragraph 35). However, safety method statements may be incorporated into the permit-to-work system.

34 Employers should ensure the safety method statement, whether it is prepared by their own staff or outside contractors, is clear, concise and contains the following information:

(a) a description of the task and where it is to be carried out;

(b) the sequence and method of work;

(c) the hazards identified during the risk assessment;

(d) the skills required to deal with the hazards;

(e) the precautions necessary to control the hazards;

(f) references to specific safety procedures covering known hazards;

(g) details of any isolations and any related control procedures;

(h) details of tools and equipment to be used;

(i) method of disposal of waste and debris; and

(j) details of the state or condition in which the plant or equipment will be left at the end of the activity.

ACOP

Permit-to-work

35 Where the proposed work is identified as a high risk activity, employers should ensure that strict controls are in place and that the work is only carried out against previously agreed safety procedures by implementing a permit-to-work system.

Guidance

36 High risk activities are those where the foreseeable consequences of an error or an omission could result in immediate and serious injuries, for example an explosion or a fire that immediately affects people or traps them. They will normally include:

Guidance

(a) hot work on or in any plant and equipment (including containers and pipes, eg storage tank, drum, cylinder, silo, pipeline, fuel tank etc) remaining in situ that contains or may have contained a dangerous substance;

(b) carrying out hot work or introducing ignition sources in areas that are normally designated as hazardous due to the presence of an explosive atmosphere - this includes places classified as hazardous under regulation 7(1) of DSEAR;[1]

(c) hot work in the vicinity of plant or equipment containing a dangerous substance where a potential outbreak of fire caused by the work might spread to threaten them;

(d) entry into, and work in, a confined space which contains or has contained a dangerous substance or where the work activity introduces a dangerous substance into the confined space; and

(e) opening or breaking into plant and equipment, or disconnecting a fixed joint that contains or has contained a dangerous substance (excluding routine activities such as charging, discharging and sampling which are themselves covered by other standard operating procedures).

37 A permit-to-work is a documented system that authorises certain people to carry out specific work within a specified time frame. It sets out the precautions required to complete the work safely and should be based on a risk assessment. It will describe what work will be done and how it will be done; the latter can be detailed in an attached safety method statement (see paragraph 30). The permit-to-work requires declarations from the person authorising the work and from the person carrying out the work. Where necessary it will also require a declaration from those involved in shift handover procedures or extensions to the work. Finally, where plant is to be put back into service, it will require a declaration from the originator of the permit that the work is complete and that the plant is ready for normal use.

38 The permit-to-work should be clearly laid out and avoid statements which could be misleading and ambiguous. It should be designed to allow for use in unusual circumstances and detail procedures if the work needs to be suspended for any reason.

39 As well as detailing the precautions that need to be taken to prevent a fire or explosion, the permit-to-work should cover the precautions that are required to control health hazards and where necessary the hazards arising from entry into confined spaces; electric shock; high pressure systems; and contact with moving equipment.

ACOP

40 Employers should ensure that a permit-to-work is only issued by a responsible person who is sufficiently knowledgeable about permit systems and the work processes, including the materials, processes, plant and equipment associated with the proposed work, to be able to identify all the potential hazards and precautions.

41 Employers, when operating a permit-to-work system, should ensure that:

(a) there is clear identification of who may authorise particular jobs and who is responsible for specifying the necessary precautions, who is responsible for checking that these precautions are followed and who is responsible for auditing the permit system;

ACOP

(b) everyone involved in the permit-to-work system, including supervisors, and those undertaking the work activity, including employees, contractors and sub-contractors are aware of their responsibilities and duties under the system and understand them;

(c) those issuing, using, monitoring and auditing the permits are provided with the proper training and instruction; and

(d) there is monitoring and auditing of the system to ensure it works as intended and to ensure everyone involved in the system is held accountable for the responsibilities assigned to them.

42 Where the activities of contractors, sub-contractors or the self-employed require risks to be controlled by a permit-to-work system operated by on-site personnel, the employer of the contracting company should ensure that:

(a) all supervisors and employees are made aware of and understand the permit-to-work system;

(b) all supervisors and employees understand the procedures and any specific arrangements made for a job, area or location in which they are to work.

43 Where the activities of contractors, sub-contractors or the self-employed require risks to be controlled through their own permit-to-work system the employer of the contracting company should comply with the requirements of paragraphs 40 and 41. Where the risks arising from this work may be affected by the presence or activities of others the employer should inform on-site personnel accordingly.

Guidance

44 For high risk activities carried out off-site the person authorising the work may be a member of the team carrying out the work. In such cases they must be properly trained to identify the hazards and precautions and in operating the permit-to-work procedures as detailed in paragraphs 40 and 41 above.

Activities involving hot work

45 Hot work is considered to be any procedure which may involve or have the potential to generate sufficient heat, sparks or flame to cause a fire. Hot work will include welding, flame cutting, soldering, brazing, grinding, and using disc cutters and other similar equipment.

ACOP

Eliminate the need for hot work

46 Wherever reasonably practicable employers should eliminate the need for hot work by the use of other processes that do not involve the application of heat or the generation of heat or sparks.

Guidance

47 The use of cold cutting equipment including low speed drills, saws and chisels may not be considered to be hot work but they may still create sparks or hot surfaces with the potential to ignite explosive atmospheres. Their use, therefore, should be assessed and controlled as for any other potential ignition source (see the DSEAR ACOP, *Control and mitigation measures*[5]).

Guidance

Preparation and procedures for hot work

48 Where it is not reasonably practicable to avoid hot work on plant or equipment that has contained a dangerous substance, regulation 6(3) requires the employer to apply appropriate measures, so far as is reasonably practicable, to control the fire and explosion risks.

ACOP

Cleaning and gas-freeing plant for hot work

49 Before hot work is carried out, employers should ensure, where reasonably practicable, that plant and equipment is made safe by adequate cleaning in order to eliminate any residual dangerous substances.

Guidance

50 Cleaning should be carried out to eliminate the presence of dangerous substances before hot work is carried out. For liquids, gases and solids that contain volatile residues the plant or equipment should be isolated from all sources of dangerous substances and ventilated to remove flammable vapours. The plant or equipment should then be thoroughly cleaned to ensure that all residues have been removed. Non-volatile solid residues can normally be cleaned from plant and equipment without the need for gas-freeing.

51 For very large tanks, for example on ships, it may not be reasonably practicable to thoroughly clean the whole of the tank or to inert the enclosed spaces before repairs or other activity involving hot work. In these cases, the areas around and below the proposed repair site should be cleaned back to an extent assessed as adequate by a competent person. The competent person and all those carrying out the work will need to be experienced and trained for this type of work and carry out a detailed assessment to determine the extent of the area that needs to be cleaned.

ACOP

52 Plant and equipment should be inspected and the atmospheres inside monitored by a competent person before commencing the hot work activity to ensure it is safe.

Guidance

53 The competent person will need to ensure that the surfaces have been cleaned of all residues of dangerous substances and that there are no significant amounts trapped or held in any voids, crevices or absorbent components of the plant. The competent person should also ensure by monitoring the atmosphere within the plant or equipment that it is free from all flammable gases and vapours. To be safe for hot work the concentration of any dangerous substances should be less than 1% of their lower explosion limit (LEL).

54 Isolating, cleaning and gas-freeing plant and equipment are all hazardous operations and will require their own assessments and appropriate safety procedures to be implemented before they are carried out.

55 Even when plant has been cleaned and gas-freed there is the possibility that flammable gases or vapours may re-occur during the hot work activity. The competent person will therefore need to assess the requirements for any further monitoring of the atmosphere throughout the work activity and whether this should be carried out continuously or periodically.

56 Where it is not reasonably practicable to eliminate dangerous substances by adequate cleaning techniques the employer must implement measures to control the fire and explosion risks arising from the hot work activity.

Guidance

Inerting

57 As an alternative to cleaning and gas-freeing, fire and explosion risks can be controlled by inerting. This technique can be applied where plant and equipment has been emptied of dangerous substances but, because it is difficult or impracticable to clean the plant adequately, residual amounts of materials still remain. Even residual amounts of dangerous substances present a fire and explosion risk as they can easily ignite or form explosive atmospheres during hot work.

58 Inerting techniques use water, nitrogen foam, nitrogen gas, combustion gas or carbon dioxide to reduce the oxygen content in the plant to below the levels that combustion can occur. Such techniques are therefore only applicable to dangerous substances that are flammable, highly flammable or extremely flammable or to substances that can create an explosive atmosphere on heating. They are not applicable to dangerous substances which are oxidising materials or chemically unstable and can react without the presence of atmospheric oxygen to give rise to hazardous heat or pressure effects.

ACOP

59 Where inerting is used as a control measure during hot work, adequate inert material should be added and maintained at the necessary level for the duration of the work, to ensure that the atmosphere in the plant or equipment cannot support combustion, or that any free volume is sufficiently small that any explosion within this will not pose a danger.

Guidance

60 Inerting techniques can give rise to hazardous situations if insufficient inert material is added to plant and equipment to achieve and maintain a non-combustible atmosphere or if people are exposed to dangerous quantities of toxic or asphyxiating gases and vapours. Further information can be found in *Safe work in confined spaces*.[10] Additionally, the dangerous substance displaced during the inerting process may accumulate in areas outside the plant and equipment to give rise to other unseen health and safety hazards. These techniques should only be undertaken by competent persons using appropriate measuring equipment, systems of work and safety equipment.

61 Before commencing hot work on plant that has been inerted with nitrogen gas, carbon dioxide or combustion gas the atmosphere should be checked at various levels, using a correctly calibrated oxygen meter, to ensure that the oxygen content has been reduced to below the planned level. Employers should also assess any risk to health from inerting techniques under COSHH 2002.[8]

ACOP

Working on live plant

62 In exceptional circumstances hot work can be carried out on plant or equipment containing a dangerous substance without cleaning or inerting. Such techniques are only applicable to plant or equipment containing liquids or gases and are not suitable for plant containing dangerous substances which are solids, dusts or explosives or that contain liquid or gaseous oxygen. Where it is intended to carry out hot work on plant or equipment that still contains a dangerous substance the employer must ensure that:

(a) there is sufficient liquid or gas within the plant to prevent air or oxygen from entering and forming an explosive atmosphere;

ACOP

(b) flames or heat will only be applied to the outside surface of the plant;

(c) the plant cannot fail or leak as a result of the hot work activity and allow liquid or gas to escape and ignite;

(d) the gas or liquid composition cannot change to become an explosive atmosphere during the hot work;

(e) sufficient control can be exercised over the movement of materials into or out of that plant and any associated plant or equipment;

(f) substances or residues present in the plant cannot undergo any reaction or decomposition leading to a dangerous increase in pressure or attack of the metal;

(g) these techniques are only carried out under a strict permit-to-work system (see paragraph 35);

(h) all personnel involved in planning and carrying out the work and supervising it are competent and trained in appropriate procedures and fire and explosion hazards; and

(i) there are no explosive atmospheres around the work area arising from that plant or other work activities.

Guidance

63   The specified conditions above prevent a fire or explosion by ensuring that the contents of the plant are kept above their higher explosion limit and that the hot work is only carried out on the outside of the plant.

64   Working on live plant has a greater potential to give rise to fires and explosions as a result of incorrect procedures or human error. A number of procedures using hot work on live plant have been developed and used safely. These procedures are detailed in guidance published by HSE and the Institution of Gas Engineers and Managers and if followed correctly will provide a safe method of working.

Using gas welding and cutting equipment

65   The gaseous fuels and oxygen used in gas welding and cutting equipment are dangerous substances and regulations 5 and 6 therefore require employers to assess the risks arising from their use and to implement appropriate control measures.

ACOP

66   The assessment should include consideration of:

(a) leaks of oxygen or fuel gases and the practicality of odorising bulk oxygen supplies;

(b) possible build up of oxygen or fuel gases in confined spaces and the practicality of using gas detection monitors (a confined space is defined by the Confined Spaces Regulations 1997);

(c) fires and explosions inside the equipment caused by:

- flashback from the blowpipe;
- decomposition of acetylene; and
- high-pressure oxygen;

ACOP

(d) safe storage of gas cylinders both during use and when not in use; and

(e) fire spread to other combustible materials.

67 Employers must implement measures to control the risk of fires and explosions arising from gaseous fuels and oxygen used in gas welding and cutting equipment. These measures will include:

(a) provision of appropriate equipment that has been designed and constructed to recognised standards. This will include the provision of hoses with properly made hose end connections, regulators, gauges, non-return valves, flame arresters and, where appropriate, pressure relief valves;

(b) inspecting and maintaining equipment in accordance with the manufacturer's instructions;

(c) locating gas cylinders in safe areas both during use and when not in use. During use, gas cylinders should be located in well-ventilated areas away from heat sources and where they cannot be accidentally or deliberately damaged. Gas cylinders should not normally be used within confined spaces (for example during ship repair). Where their use cannot be avoided, special precautions, for example local exhaust ventilation, need to be taken to prevent the dangerous build up of gases or fumes. Where cylinders are used in this situation, supply valves should be securely closed when they are left unattended for short periods of time - such as for tea breaks or toilet breaks;

(d) routing gas hoses or pipes through areas where they are not easily damaged or near to heat sources;

(e) where moveable gas hoses or pipes are used or routed through confined spaces they should be removed to a well ventilated area at the end of the working period and at every significant break in the work (such as meal breaks). Where pipes and hoses cannot be removed, they should be disconnected from the gas at a point outside the confined space and their contents safely vented;

(f) provision of appropriate training, instruction and supervision to ensure correct operating procedures are followed; and

(g) taking appropriate fire precautions.

ACOP

References and further reading

References

1 *The Dangerous Substances and Explosive Atmospheres Regulations 2002* SI 2002/2776 The Stationery Office 2002 ISBN 0 11 042957 5

2 *Dangerous Substances and Explosive Atmospheres. Dangerous Substances and Explosive Atmospheres Regulations. Approved Code of Practice and guidance* L138 HSE Books 2003 ISBN 0 7176 2203 7

3 *Design of plant, equipment and workplaces. Dangerous Substances and Explosive Atmospheres Regulations 2002. Approved Code of Practice and guidance* L134 HSE Books 2003 ISBN 0 7176 2199 5

4 *Storage of dangerous substances. Dangerous Substances and Explosive Atmospheres Regulations 2002. Approved Code of Practice and guidance* L135 HSE Books 2003 ISBN 0 7176 2200 2

5 *Control and mitigation measures. Dangerous Substances and Explosive Atmospheres Regulations 2002. Approved Code of Practice and guidance* L136 HSE Books 2003 ISBN 0 7176 2201 0

6 *Unloading petrol from road tankers. Dangerous Substances and Explosive Atmospheres Regulations 2002. Approved Code of Practice and guidance* L133 HSE Books 2003 ISBN 0 7176 2197 9

7 *Fire and explosion: How safe is your workplace? A short guide to the Dangerous Substances and Explosive Atmospheres Regulations* Leaflet INDG370 HSE Books 2002 (single copy free or priced packs of 5 ISBN 0 7176 2589 3)

8 *The Control of Substances Hazardous to Health Regulations 2002* SI 2002/2677 The Stationery Office 2002 ISBN 0 11 042919 2

9 *The Confined Spaces Regulations 1997* SI 1997/1713 The Stationery Office 1997 ISBN 0 11 064643 6

10 *Safe work in confined spaces. Confined Spaces Regulations 1997. Approved Code of Practice, Regulations and guidance* L101 HSE Books 1997 ISBN 0 7176 1405 0

Further reading

Permit-to-work systems Leaflet INDG98(rev3) HSE Books 1997 (single copy free or priced packs of 15 ISBN 0 7176 1331 3)

Guidance on permit-to-work systems in the petroleum industry (Third edition) Guidance HSE Books 1997 ISBN 0 7176 1281 3

Safe use and handling of flammable liquids HSG140 HSE Books 1996 ISBN 0 7176 0967 7

The cleaning and gas-freeing of tanks containing flammable residues CS15 HSE Books 1985 ISBN 0 7176 1365 8

Tank Cleaning Safety Code. Model Code of Safe Practice Part 16 2nd edition Institute of Petroleum 1996 ISBN 0 471 97096 4 available from Portland Customer Services, Commerce Way, Whitehall Industrial Estate, Colchester CO2 8HP, tel: 01206 796 351, fax: 01206 799 331, e-mail: sales@portland-services.com, website: www.portlandpress.com

The safe isolation of plant and equipment Guidance HSE Books 1997 ISBN 0 7176 0871 9

The Dangerous Substances and Explosive Atmospheres Regulations 2002. A short guide for the offshore industry HSE Offshore Division Operations Notice 58 available online at http://www.hse.gov.uk/hid/osd/notices/on_index.htm

The Equipment and Protective Systems Intended for use in Potentially Explosive Atmospheres Regulations 1996. A short guide for the offshore industry HSE Offshore Division Operations Notice 59 available online at http://www.hse.gov.uk/hid/osd/notices/on_index.htm

Guidance for the design, construction, modification and maintenance of petrol filling stations Association for Petroleum and Explosives Administration/Institute of Petroleum 1999 ISBN 0 85293 217 0 available from Portland Customer Services, Commerce Way, Whitehall Industrial Estate, Colchester CO2 8HP, tel: 01206 796 351, fax: 01206 799 331, e-mail: sales@portland-services.com, website: www.portlandpress.com

BS 6187:2000 *Code of practice for demolition* British Standards Institution

The safe use of compressed gases in welding, flame cutting and allied processes HSG139 HSE Books 1997 ISBN 0 7176 0680 5

Safe working practices to ensure the integrity of gas pipelines and associated installations IGE/SR/18 2nd edition Institution of Gas Engineers and Managers 2002 available from Institution of Gas Engineers and Managers, Charnwood Wing, Ashby Road, Loughborough, Leicester LE11 3GH, tel: 01509 282728, fax: 01509 283193

External joint repairs in gas distribution systems IGE/SR/19 Institution of Gas Engineers and Managers 1990 available from Institution of Gas Engineers and Managers, Charnwood Wing, Ashby Road, Loughborough, Leicester LE11 3GH, tel: 01509 282728, fax: 01509 283193

Gas installation pipework, boosters and compressors on industrial and commercial premises IGE/UP/2 Institution of Gas Engineers and Managers 1994 available from Institution of Gas Engineers and Managers, Charnwood Wing, Ashby Road, Loughborough, Leicester LE11 3GH, tel: 01509 282728, fax: 01509 283193